Why Women Should Pray

Why Women Should Pray
Copyright © 2020 Salome B. Ikem

All rights reserved. No part of this book may be reproduced (except for inclusion in reviews), disseminated, or utilized in any form or by any means, electronic or mechanical, including photocopying, recording, or in any information storage and retrieval system, or the Internet/World Wide Web without written permission from the author or publisher.

Book design by:
Arbor Services, Inc.
www.arborservices.co/

Printed in the United States of America

Why Women Should Pray
Salome B. Ikem

1. Title 2. Author 3. Self-Help

Library of Congress Control Number: 2020921099
ISBN 13: 978-0-578-79139-5

Why Women Should Pray

MINISTER SALOME IKEM

To my God, my creator, and my heavenly Father, who awakened me to life and taught me how to pray and build a strong, loving relationship with him. Humbled, I open my heart and soul to the divine Lord, eager to accept his will.

To all women who pray, and to those women who, upon reading my words, will become available to experience joy and comfort in speaking to God in prayer as I do. You too will learn the value of faith and patience in awaiting God's timing.

Contents

ACKNOWLEDGMENTS 1
TESTIMONY OF A MIRACLE 2
TESTIMONY OF AN ANSWERED PRAYER 3
TESTIMONY ON HOW I MET MY HUSBAND 5
INTRODUCTION 7

CHAPTER ONE
    Power in a Woman's Prayer 11

CHAPTER TWO
    Every Woman Is a Mother 16

CHAPTER THREE
    We Pray Because We Want to Be Holy 21

CHAPTER FOUR
    Women Are Carriers of the Gospel 26

CHAPTER FIVE
    We Pray Because We Have Rebellious Children 30

CHAPTER SIX
    We Pray Because We Are What God Said We Are 34

CHAPTER SEVEN
    We Pray Because We Have Challenges 39

CHAPTER EIGHT
    We Pray Because We Love 43

CHAPTER NINE
    We Pray Because We Need God 48

AFTERWORD 52

ACKNOWLEDGMENTS

I thank God for his grace and inspiration that empowered me to conceive and write *Why Women Should Pray*, my second book. Without his presence in my life I would have neither the knowledge nor the experience to pen my own testimony to the power of prayer.

To my darling husband, Rev. Dr. Akaeze Ikem, I offer special thanks for always standing by me through the storms and sunny days alike, and for sharing my faith commitment to bring God's message to all.

I am grateful for my four beautiful children: my three sons, Nnamdi Mark, Chinedu Karl, and Chison Samuel, and my daughter, Ngozi Franca—each a uniquely amazing gift from the Lord, blessing my marriage. For you I have limitless love. You have always encouraged me to push forward to be a better woman and to live my life as a devout Christian role model for you to love, respect, and emulate.

I extend my gratitude to all the members of Jesus Without Borders International Church for your support and loyal solidarity. I appreciate every one of you who faithfully joined me in prayer: Mr. & Mrs. Shirley Sanders, Mrs. Janet Happoldt, Christ is Lord International Church, Woodbridge Christian Church, and Gilgal Fellowship International. Please receive my heartfelt thanks for accompanying me on my journey. My prayers are your prayers. May God grant you abundant blessings, in appreciation and with gratitude and love.

TESTIMONY OF A MIRACLE

After two major surgeries due to ectopic pregnancies, God felt my pains and answered my prayers by giving me a miracle.

Miracle? Yes, miracles always happen according to God's timing. Fearful of past pains and disappointments, I always worried about a pregnancy. However, despite my fears, God was working behind the scenes for my happiness.

Suddenly and unexpectedly, I found myself pregnant without realizing it. I was suffering pain and discomfort on and off, and my visit to urgent care confirmed I was pregnant. A thorough examination revealed it was not ectopic. I knew I would continue to pray.

In my thirty-seventh week, I gave birth. This time the pain from surgery was joyful. I had prayed and the Lord heard my words. Now I give thanks for the miracle of life I received.

~ Anita Seton

TESTIMONY OF AN ANSWERED PRAYER

Praise the Lord. My name is Hawa Brown, and this is my testimony. I just want to express my gratitude to God for how far he has brought me. I've been married since 2004, and we all know when we get married, our next expectation is to have children. My husband and I prayed for this favor. We waited on God from 2004 through 2019, trusting in the Lord and praying, because he says, "We shall pray without ceasing." He does not want us ever to give up, and I know we should hold on. Obedient to the word of God, I obeyed.

I am grateful to God for the strength and determination not to give up. The doctor said it wasn't possible for us to have children. However, I knew that with God, all things are possible! And I am so grateful unto God because in his own timing and in his own due season, through prayer and fasting, he blessed me.

I thank God for the servant of God, Pastor Ikem, who stood by me on my eleventh anniversary and prayed along with us. In faith he declared a word concerning the fruit of the womb, emphasizing that the Lord was going to bless me with a son. I just want to tell God how appreciative I am for my papa. I am so beholden for my papa apostle, with whom I came in contact. In faith, he also declared the same word: The Lord was going to bless me with the fruit of the womb—a son.

Brothers and sisters, I hope in the word of God. Today I am a living testimony of faith and trust. God said one thousand years is like a day before him. Truly the word came to pass in August of 2019 when the Lord blessed me with the creation of life, and by the grace of God on March 31, 2020, the baby saw the light of day! I am so indebted to share my testimony and encourage you as children of God to always live in faith and never give up. Let us continue to be patient in our season, and the Lord will fulfill what he promised in your life. The Lord is truth and knows not how to lie, and therefore as the Son of God, he need never repent. "Ask and you shall receive." All that he says concerning our lives will come to pass.

I hope my testimony will reassure any woman who doubts that Jesus is alive. He is all we need and all we should desire. As promised, he is a God who answers prayers according to his time and season. Walk in faith, remain in the Lord, and never abandon hope. Keep believing and you will receive. Amen.

~ Hawa Brown

TESTIMONY ON HOW I MET MY HUSBAND

I was at the tail end of finishing my high school studies, not thinking of getting involved in any form of relationship, when my now husband sent someone to tell me that he was interested in having me as his fiancée. Eventually I met him and told him the devil was using him in this moment and that he should concentrate on his studies. We met three years after the discussion, and he told me was tired of waiting and was thinking of changing his mind on the issue of a relationship. However, he decided to ask me about his proposal several years earlier. I told him to give me some time to go and seek the face of God. I had to be sure this was his will for me because I was committed to God in all things, always knowing I didn't want to enter into any relationship that would not lead to marriage.

One night I dreamt of someone telling me I should accept the proposal because he is the will of God for me. I decided to say yes. Fortunately, we were attending the same church. Guess what? I started to hide from him. One Sunday, as the closing prayer was being said, I rushed out of the church so he would not see me. But God was busy showing me the way, and one faithful afternoon my future husband approached and held my hand. I could not run away again. He told me that if I was not interested in his proposal, I should inform him so that he could make other plans. I went home that day and prayed. Later I wrote him a letter expressing how much I loved him. I also told him that since I had never been in a relationship before, would he please be patient with me. He agreed and began to court me with the intention of marriage. The will of God came to be. We have been together as husband and wife for thirteen years, and have been blessed with two beautiful children. Prayer is powerful. God listens to a woman's prayer.

~ Minister Marian K. Bangura

INTRODUCTION

Born on November 4, 1978, and reared in the Atlantic Port City of Freetown, Sierra Leone, I studied childhood education and embarked on an academic career. Following my passion for engaging youngsters in learning, I undertook a teaching position at an English school and later at the American International School of Conakry, Guinea's capital city.

From early on, an unwavering faith powered my life. At the turn of the third millennium in 2001, God had Rev. Dr. Akaeze Ikem cross my path in a meeting that eventually led to marriage. God blessed us with three beautiful, healthy sons. Nevertheless, unknown to us at the time, our family was not yet complete: All in the Lord's timing. *"Be still before the Lord and wait patiently for him"* Psalm 37:7.

Six years afterward, united in a deep faith commitment, together with the Holy Spirit we founded our church, Christ4Crisis Ministry (Jesus without Borders). Ours was a ministry dedicated to evangelism and the care of the Lord's less privileged little ones in Africa.

Obedient servants of our creator, we took to heart the words of Jesus: *"Therefore, whoever takes the lowly position of this child is the greatest in the kingdom of heaven. And whoever welcomes one such child in my name welcomes me"* Matthew 18:4–5. A helping hand was extended to every child in various stages of urgency. Their needs were and continue to be urgent for nutritional food, fresh drinking water, spiritual guidance, tutoring, and medical attention—needs that seem to grow exponentially.

In 2013, after much prayer and reflection, we decided to emigrate from Conakry, Guinea, to the United States. God was sending us on a different journey. Although the continent was now different, the mission remained intact. Thus, we founded Christ4Crisis Church in Woodbridge, Virginia, with an even more profound mission to carry the message and story of Christianity to all desirous of knowing the Father, Son, and Holy Spirit.

Hardships and adversity were never a stranger to me, though feelings of hopelessness and despair were. Sometimes the paths of my journey were obstructed. I carried an inconsolable sadness for having left my three sons in Africa. But I never stopped believing. Why? Because I had PRAYER. My time spent with the Lord and my words with him kept me focused, optimistic, comforted, encouraged, empowered, and secure of the path I was following as a Christian woman, wife, mother, and ordained minister with twenty years' experience in the teaching profession.

With the birth of my daughter and the arrival of my three sons, my family was complete and united. Through it all, PRAYER was the glue that kept me grounded and strengthened my relationship with the Lord. I now understand the power of raising my voice to the Lord.

In gratitude, I wrote *Why Women Should Pray* to share with other women the wisdom God granted to me. Praise be to God Almighty—my creator, my savior, my comforter, my advocate, my strength, and my bearer of truth. May every woman who prays discover the glory, intercession, and assistance in blessings received. Have faith and love instead of chastising others, and never cease to PRAY.

CHAPTER ONE

Power in a Woman's Prayer

I urge, then, first of all, that petitions, prayers, intercession and thanksgiving be made for all people.
~ *1 Timothy 2:1*

Why Women Should Pray
I call on you, my God, for you will answer me: turn your ear to me and hear my prayer. ~ *Psalm 17:6*

We pray because, as women, our faith assures us that we will be heard! In Isaiah 41:10 is written: *"So do not fear, for I am with you; Do not be dismayed, for I am your God; I strengthen you, and help you; I will uphold you with my victorious right hand."*

Clear and concise, I do believe the Lord's words do not yield to doubt: *"Do not fear, for I am with you."* Loving and kind, the Lord reassures us of his omnipresence as we live through our days and evenings.

Different cycles in a woman's life present diverse challenges and sorrows, and often a varied array of joys, frustrations, and unsettling situations. During these moments we are urged to turn to our divine creator. Why? Because as nurturers, bringing up and fostering the creatures God bequeaths to us—as the Lord was to

Mary—he offers special support, assistance, and his healing graces for strength in times of distress.

Moreover, impregnated not solely with the seeds of life, we as women also carry in our wombs, through the intervention of the Holy Spirit, the words of the Gospel. In reading Luke 7:11–12, we see the special place a mother occupies in the heart of Christ. *"Soon afterward Jesus went to a town named Nain accompanied by His disciples and a large crowd. And when he arrived at the gate of the town a funeral procession was coming out."*

Why did I cite this passage? Simply stated, in this reading we learn that Jesus witnessed a prominent funeral procession in Nain in which the entire town participated. Attentive, he observed not only the young men and women weeping, but noticed the tears of the pastors and apostles. The fathers wept; the children's faces were stained with tears; a striking sadness overcame the faces of all the mourners.

The deceased was the only son of a widow. Though saddened by the tears of the men, women, and children weeping for their loss, the Lord was enveloped in a deep compassion for the woman living in fullness her vocation as a MOTHER. What takes precedence is the heart of the Lord moved by the tears of a mother, not solely at the funeral of Nain but, as the Bible demonstrates, whenever a woman prays to the Son of God for her marriage, her family, or her home.

Although the energy in Nain was heavy with the stifling grief of loss, nothing seemed to call the Lord to action until his eyes rested on the mother of the deceased boy. Jesus forged through the crowd, making his way directly to the bereaved mother, in spite of the dictates of the culture of the time with a prevailing attitude that disregarded women as insignificant individuals who, therefore, were neither encouraged to pray nor read the Bible—a culture that failed to sanction men approaching women in public spaces.

When the Lord saw her, his heart went out to her and he said, "Don't cry." ~ Luke 7:13

What exactly happened? In a few words, the heart of Jesus was overcome with compassion for the widow who had just suffered a devastating tragedy. Deeply touched, he was stirred to perform a miracle. And thus, the young man was raised from the dead and returned to his mother.

Like a Mother, God Loves, Protects, and Defends his Children

What does this parable tell us about the Lord's empathy for women? The response is in his own words inscribed in Jeramiah 33:3: *"Call to me and I will answer you, and tell you great and unsearchable things you do not know."* Who could possibly dispute this invocation? Clearly this is an invitation summoning women to pray.

God's role is similar to that of a mother. As a mother protects, upholds, and defends her children, likewise God protects, keeping us under the shadow of his wing: *"I will take refuge in the shadow of your wings until the disaster has passed"* Psalm 57:1. We find refuge there, and can hide there until the danger is over. A mother's role is so vital that a father's prayers will not be answered if he dishonors or disrespects her: *'Husbands, in the same way be considerate as you live with your wives, and treat them with respect as the weaker partner and as heirs with you of the gracious gift of life, so that nothing will hinder your prayers"* 1 Peter 3:7.

Because God favors mothers, they are also the most attacked persons in the home. The devil is terrified of mothers. Yet the Lord has given mothers the grace and resilience to overcome any situation.

Mothers' Tears before the Lord

Still today, mothers who cry before the Lord for their families, for their marriages, and for their homes move the heart of God. Why? Because they are creatures *after God's own heart.* However, when temptation surfaces and doubts arise, leading to a pause in prayer, their families (especially their children) suffer consequences. In these instances, we need God's light to sustain us. *"In him was life; and the life was the light of men"* John 1:4.

Once Satan gains a foothold, he starts to destroy the rightful place of the Lord as the anchor of the home. Ruthlessly and unscrupulously, Satan tries to twist and mold women into his allies, as he did with Eve in the Garden of Eden. However, demonic strongholds get demolished with a mother's prayer.

"Did God really say you must not eat from any tree in the garden?" Genesis 3:1. Satan's words to Eve were cynical and deceptive; his way was that of an evil and immoral creature, a being who behaved with great wickedness. But let us not forget his convincing nature brought her to betray the divine order leading to a grave offense—sin and chaos in the world.

Likewise, when a mother doubts the supremacy of prayer, all havoc breaks loose, interrupting the serenity and harmony of children and parents. Thus, the family begins to tremble like a city trapped in an earthquake, eventually slipping into the quicksand of transgression. Nevertheless, there is hope. Only a mother's prayers to the Lord will open the door for him to enter and establish order to an unrestrained household.

"Ask and it will be given to you" is the Lord's promise recorded in Matthew 7:7—a commitment that encourages you as wife and mother to ask the Lord to cross the threshold of your home. In your request and in your prayer, the presence of the Lord in your life will strengthen. More importantly, your very word is the one arm that declaws Satan, pushing him into impotency.

Although the first woman fell to the knavish temptation, she need not have a following. Why? Because Satan fears mothers who pray. Prayer is powerful. A mother's words are inviolable.

The far-reaching influence of a mother's prayer does not exclude the role of husbands and fathers in worshiping the Lord. Quite the contrary: *"Husbands, in the same way be considerate as you live with your wives; and treat them with respect as the weaker partner and as heirs with you of the gracious gift of life, so that nothing will hinder your prayers"* 1 Peter 3:7.

Men, beware—the Lord will not respond to the prayers of a disrespectful husband and father who fails to carry honor and respect in his heart for his wife and the mother of his children. Remember, intercessory prayer has no limits.

CHAPTER TWO

Every Woman Is a Mother

She speaks with wisdom, and faithful instruction is on her tongue. She watches over the affairs of her household and does not eat the bread of idleness.
~ Proverbs 31:26–27

A Woman Is a Nurturer

The man called his wife's name Eve, because she was the mother of all living. ~ Genesis 3:20.

Did you ever ponder just what it means to be a Christian woman and nurturer according to the divine creator's design? And did you ever ask yourself if the vocation of motherhood is limited to the exclusive fostering of children either personally birthed or adopted? Sometimes definitions seem rather limiting, don't they?

Are there answers to these inquiries? In reality, just one: the responses to life's most intricate unknowns are found wrapped in biblical verses. But if we don't keep our Bibles close at hand and easy to access, I am fearful life's questions will be saved in the impenetrable folder labeled unsolvable mysteries.

Let us move along and examine the vocation of motherhood. Mothering means to nurse with care and affection. This implies that as women, we should always be willing and ready to nurse and exercise care and concern for all around us through prayer and good works. People depend on us, our husbands rely on us; likewise for our children, family members, friends, and colleagues.

What are the qualities of a devoted mother? A woman should have the ability to inspire, the willingness to commit to hard work, the merits of patience, humility, perseverance, and tolerance. She should possess a kind and forgiving heart, simplicity, compassion, and understanding. These characteristics are not only essential values but serve as the foundation of a good Christian life.

Of course, most important is love: A mother's love for her children cannot be described in words. It is a deep, all-consuming, unconditional love. Her heart should be open, her spirit willing, her intentions focused on her children, and her mind equipped to accept the Lord's challenges with her availability to pray and reflect on the Word of God.

Like the Lord, women are first and foremost nurturers. In the apostle Paul's words to Timothy, we understand the strong and everlasting influence of women in the lives not only of their family members but in all whom they chance to encounter during their life journey. *"I am reminded of your sincere faith, which first lived in your grandmother Lois and in your mother Eunice and, I am persuaded, now lives in you also"* 2 Timothy 1:5.

Mothers' Dependance on God

A mother living in faith never fails to acknowledge her reliance on God in mothering her children and others. She is fully aware that a life of full commitment to God's Word gives her the encouragement, strength, and nourishment to undertake challenging days when children misbehave or are anxious, and her support is needed. With God beside her, she does not feel discouraged. Pausing at various moments to pray for her children, she allows a special divine guidance to intervene. *"If any of you lacks wisdom, you should ask God, who gives generously to all without finding fault, and it will be given to you"* James 1:5. Aren't these words a consolation? Pray for wisdom in rearing your children: the Lord does not deny the prayers of a mother.

A Woman Is a Warrior
You armed me with strength for battle; you humbled my adversaries before me ~ Psalm 18:39.

Actually, mothers incorporate diverse facets in their spiritual selves—that distinctive uniqueness we share with the divine image of Christ, the supreme nurturer who cared for all of humanity.

Sometimes love is just not enough. Why? Because in order to be a virtuous mother, a woman must also be a protector, a friend, and a disciplinarian, a firm disciplinarian who rules with kindness and love while attending to all the needs of the children the Lord placed in her heart. Selfless, she sacrifices many of her personal wants and needs for the wants and needs of her children.

Always be mindful that Satan struggles to weaken and sabotage all that the Lord gives us to raise our children in his graces. But if we live and pray over his indestructible word in the Bible, we will triumph. I cannot say enough about prayer. It is, after all, synonymous with victory.

As mothers, we protect through our prayers, and we pray because we wish to tell the Lord that we are always ready to make sacrifices for the welfare and defense of our children. *"The weapons we fight with are not the weapons of the world. On the contrary, they have divine power to demolish strongholds. We demolish arguments and every pretension that sets itself up against the knowledge of God, and we take captive every thought to make it obedient to Christ"* 2 Corinthians 10:4–5.

We hold our children safely in the sanctuary of our arms and hearts. Yet, although we are primarily nurturers, we are likewise warriors. Undeniably, we are a powerful presence here to fight for those we love, cherish, and care for. We must, however, never lose sight of the truth: our maternal prayer is compelling—it carries to our children special divine favor and encourages them to walk along the righteous path.

A mother in prayer with the Lord provides security for her children. Every word from her lips is both an assurance of protection and a defense. For us as mothers, this same prayer prepares us to stand tall and confront the adversary in our spiritual warfare, an evil force that seeks only to invade and take over, snatching us from the Lord. Remember, Satan detests women who pray. Make Ephesians 6:10–11 one of your battle songs. *"Finally, be strong in the Lord and in his mighty power. Put on the full armor of God, so that you can take your stand against the devil's schemes."*

Be aware that a mother is supposed to gather her children, not scatter them, speak to them with her wisdom and kindness, all while upholding biblical expectations. Above all, when the season is ripe, she will be ready to let her children take flight. *"She is clothed with strength and dignity; she can laugh at the days to come"* Proverbs 31:25.

Once again, when it's their time to fly, give the children you nurtured their wings. We witnessed, in chapter one, the Lord's compassion for a mother at the funeral of Nain. Throughout his life, Jesus felt this heartbreak for women: *"Jerusalem, Jerusalem, you who kill the prophets and stone those sent to you, how often I have longed to gather your children together, as a hen gathers her chicks under her wings, and you were not willing"* Luke 13:34.

The Lord responds to our prayers! Therefore, I cannot sufficiently emphasize the responsibility of women to be prayerful. Although as mothers we are an important point of departure, we are primarily a life giver. In Genesis 3:20 we have the confirmation of women as the bearer of life: *"Adam named his wife Eve because she would become the mother of all the living."* Let us wisely use the wisdom and gifts the Lord has given to us.

CHAPTER THREE

We Pray Because We Want to Be Holy

Rejoice always, pray continually, give thanks in all circumstances; for this is God's will for you in Christ Jesus.
~ 1 Thessalonians 5:16–18

What Is a Holy Woman?

In 1 Peter 1:16 we read the words of the Lord: "*Be holy because I am holy.*" The message is clear. As women and mothers, we are called to be holy, summoned to a holiness that expects us to honor the divine will. Though it sounds easy enough, unless we understand what exactly it means to be a holy woman, we cannot live our own holiness.

Paul says in his second epistle, "*He has saved us and called us to a holy life—not because of anything we have done but because of his own purpose and grace. This grace was given us in Christ Jesus before the beginning of time*" 2 Timothy 1:9.

The Lord repeatedly sends us challenges, many of which we do not understand. However, in those moments, having the holiness to accept and bear suffering is a way to partake in Christ's own suffering. Once again it is the story of creation. We were made in the image of God. Thus, even suffering brings special strengthening graces. Furthermore, how can we pray if we are not holy? The truth is we can't. This is why we must keep ourselves holy unto the Lord. How? By following 1 Corinthians 6:19–20, *"Do you not know that your bodies are temples of the Holy Spirit, who is in you, whom you have received from God? You are not your own, you were bought at a price. Therefore, honor God with your bodies."*

Holiness is not just a virtue but a day-to-day lifestyle. It is the way we talk, how we dress, and the attitude with which we carry ourselves and move about. Aside from a godliness of the soul, holiness involves diverse aspects of our being, the who we are—the manner in which we present ourselves and interact with our husbands, children, and all with whom we come into contact. Indeed, we should honor God with our bodies, as they do not belong to us.

Doesn't the verse in 1 Corinthians cited above confirm that we have undeniably been bought for a price? Nevertheless, *"You know that it was not with perishable things such as silver or gold that you were redeemed from the empty way of life handed down to you from your ancestors, but with the precious blood of Christ, a lamb without blemish or defect"* 1 Peter 1:18–19.

God sacrificed his only son for the salvation of mankind. Likewise, mothers are often called to renounce and give up their own wants and needs for the good of their children. Holiness is sacrifice. *"And by that will, we have been made holy through the sacrifice of the body of Jesus Christ once for all"* Hebrews 10:10.

Ordained by God before the foundation of the world, Christ's blood purchased us out of the slavery of sin and set us free forever, though it was a purchase carried out by evil men. *"This man was handed* over to you by God's deliberate plan and foreknowledge; and you, with the help of wicked men, put him to death by nailing him to the cross"* Acts 2:23.

And as Christians, our bodies are God's temple, so accordingly, we are to use them to glorify him. Therefore, if our Savior tells us that our bodies are his temple, it means they are a house of worship—the house of God. Don't we have an obligation to maintain our holiness? *"These I will bring to my holy mountain and give them joy in my house of prayer. Their burnt offerings and sacrifices will be accepted on my altar; for my house will be called a house of prayer for all nations"* Isaiah 56:7.

Since our bodies are the temple of God, we are called to a life of prayer. This same call to prayer is also seen in the New Testament, in Matthew 21:13: *"My house will be called a house of prayer, but you are making it a den of robbers."*

As women and mothers, truly wishing to please God and live our lives for him, we have to not only recognize the importance of prayer, but adopt a prayerful and holy way of life. Women should always know we are more spiritual than physical.

Just Call on God
Therefore, I tell you, whatever you ask for in prayer, believe that you have received it. ~ Mark 11:24.

Craving for prayer:
They should always pray and not give up. ~ Luke 18:1.

When children disobey, when husbands become trying and difficult, when our patience is pulled to the extreme, when we need assistance to live through the day, God expects us to come to him for the support, guidance, and strength to overcome, just as your children come to you in overwhelming moments with their pleas for help. Isn't this a proof of faith? We trust in the goodness of God and believe in his willingness to be there for us, as we are for our children. This blind faith is what sets us apart from others and gives us the godliness that makes us holy. We pray to maintain our bodies as temples of the Holy Spirit, the source and fount of wisdom. Humbled, we pray for God's assistance and collaboration in raising our children, in relating as best we can to our husbands, in understanding our coworkers, and in being the best women we can possible be. We pray for strength in adversity.

We also pray not only to give recognition and thanks to our Lord and not only for the ability to accept ourselves as extensions of the Lord, but to ask for help to reject all temptations: *"My house will be called a house of prayer"* Matthew 21:13. Only a dependence on prayer will give the strength to resist satanic enticements.

Prayer fights evil, and as women we must live with the assurance that the force of our spirit triumphs over the frailty of the body. *"When tempted, no one should say, 'God is tempting me.' For God cannot be tempted by evil, nor does he tempt anyone; but each person is tempted when they are dragged away by their own evil desire and enticed"* James 1:13–14.

As women and mothers, we must resist the temptation to let exhaustion and the interruptions of family or work deter us from our commitment to pray. Remember, prayer is the keystone of a serene life. It is not as time consuming as it may seem. Our dialogues with God need not be lengthy. All that is necessary is to keep the name of Jesus in your words. He will send the strength to face whatever challenges the day brings. It is through our whispers to the Lord that we find holiness.

CHAPTER FOUR

Women Are Carriers of the Gospel

Charm is deceitful, and beauty is vain, but a woman who fears the Lord is to be praised.
~ Proverbs 31:30

Women Evangelize First in the Home
Isaiah 52:7 gladly announces, *"How beautiful on the mountains are the feet of those who bring good news, who proclaim peace, who bring good tidings, who proclaim salvation, who say to Zion, 'Your God reigns!'"*

Evangelization begins in the home, in the family with husbands and children. As Christian women and mothers, we have an obligation to carry the word and messages of God to our offspring in the same way in which we teach them letters, numbers, and in particular life lessons.

Isn't it true that whenever a woman hears good news, she will certainly tell someone about it? Aren't we as women and mothers proud to speak good of our families? In chapter 4, verses 28–29, John the Evangelist writes: *"Then, leaving her water jar, the woman went back to the town and said to the people, 'Come, see a man who told me everything I ever did. Could this be the Messiah?'"* Women are creatures of faith. Easily we believe, and when we accept something as true, we are willing to give up everything to pursue that truth.

In so doing, we go forth and spread the gospel, we go fired up with all the enthusiasm and love placed in our hearts by the Holy Spirit the third person of the trinity, the divinity who infuses us with wisdom.

How Can Women Engage in an Evangelistic Mission?

Leaving the next day, we reached Caesarea and stayed at the house of Philip the evangelist, one of the Seven. He had four unmarried daughters who prophesied. ~ Acts 21:8–9

From the history of mankind, it is known that women by nature have always been bearers of tidings. Let us call to mind Mary's visit to Elizabeth: *"When Elizabeth heard Mary's greeting, the baby leaped in her womb, and Elizabeth was filled with the Holy Spirit. In a loud voice she exclaimed: 'Blessed are you among women, and blessed is the child you will bear!'"* Luke 1:41–42.

Don't we have a tendency to carry news to those with whom we are engaged professionally, in business, culturally, and socially? Of course, we all know this reflects the truth. So why not take it into the spiritual realm with the divine news.

First, we must realize that evangelizing is neither synonymous with preaching from the pulpit, nor a male-oriented mission. As Galatians 3:28 reassures. *"There is neither Jew nor Gentile, neither slave nor free, nor is there male and female, for you are all one in Christ Jesus."* Therefore, we cannot walk through life in spiritual silence, believing our father, husband, and sons only can spread the word of God to the four corners of the universe. In the Lord's heart there are no gender-biased roles in introducing God to humanity.

Did not the Lord appear to Mary Magdalene, entrusting her with the task of informing the apostles of his resurrection? How important was this divine action? It was the crux of Christianity, the confirmation of the prophesy fulfilled: the salvation of mankind—a total life changer! And the breaking headliner was reported by a woman, not Peter, Paul, Luke, Mark, Matthew, or John!

Every woman should make it a point to be acquainted with 2 Kings 22:15–16. It is the recount of the prophet Huldah, an envoy of God commissioned to repeat his word to Josiah: *"She said to them, this is what the Lord, the God of Israel, says: Tell the man who sent you to me, 'This is what the Lord says: I am going to bring disaster on this place and its people, according to everything written in the book the king of Judah has read.'"*

The Lord's Will for Women

These biblical events are the testimony of the Lord's will for women, not as passive bystanders, but essential disciples introducing the world of the divine narrative. He calls men and women correspondingly, because, *"There are different kinds of gifts, but the same Spirit distribute them. There are different kinds of service, but the same Lord"* 1 Corinthians 12:4–5.

Did you ever question why we are beneficiaries of these special gifts? Surely they are not ours to keep or conceal, but to share. This is clearly detailed in Romans 12, in which we are told if called to serve, we must do so; if given the wisdom to educate, we must teach; if we are blessed abundantly, we must be benefactors of our gifts; and if we are living in God's footsteps, we are obliged to bring compassion and encouragement to others.

Now we ask ourselves, how can we as women and mothers go out into the world and evangelize? How can we bring to the knowledge of others the most important story ever written? We can do so by honoring our personal quest for holiness while bringing testimony of our special relationship with the Lord. He was after all the greatest evangelizer. Scripture reaffirms that we have both a responsibility and an obligation to carry the divine word to the ears of our children.

When women share their gifts, their children learn the power of a generous heart and feel the strength of the spirit. Children are vulnerable and thirst for knowledge. Like sponges, they absorb every word from their mother's lips.

How did your children meet Jesus? How did they learn to pray? How did they discover the power of conversing with God, the comfort in a prayer? Was it not through your own prayers, even the whispered ones: was it by way of your discipleship in the family?

Devout Christians, ministers, and pastors are formed on a mother's lap. This is why the Holy Spirit awaits in the heart of a mother, his instrument of holiness; he awaits the appropriate moment to touch both the evangelizer and the evangelized. And never more than the present is there a need for evangelizers to bring light to a trying moment of darkness. Women can be and are that warming, enlightening ray in the shadows. All women are born with this amazing gift.

CHAPTER FIVE

We Pray Because We Have Rebellious Children

Charm is deceitful, and beauty is vain, but a woman who fears the Lord is to be praised.
~ Proverbs 31:30

Serenity: A Mother's Prayerful Hope
She opens her mouth with wisdom, and loving instruction is on her tongue. She watches over the ways of her household, and does not eat the bread of idleness. ~ **Proverbs 31:26–27**

Mothers are wise, we have embraced holiness, we know the value of prayer, and we pray. Why? Because we have rebellious children, because it is often the nature of a child to be disobedient and to defy. I am certain that if I ask who among us has not experienced an uncooperative child, I would not see one hand go up!

How can we overcome the hurdle of troublesome children? I will tell you how I do it. When I am fraught with worry, I keep mentioning the name of God. Follow my prayerful tactic even if resistance to your instruction has led your child to reject everything to do with God. Remember, you as a mother must put in the effort as if your influence and guidance alone is essential to resolve the issue; likewise, you must pray with the faith and certainty that only God, who created the soul of your child, has the power to calm their rebellious heart. Surely he will not abandon the child he gave immortal life to. *"Being confident of this, that he who began a good work in you will carry it on to completion until the day of Christ Jesus"* Philippians 1:6.

In Deuteronomy 6:5–7, the message to mothers is clear: *"Love the Lord your God with all your heart and with all your soul and with all your strength. These commandments that I give you today are to be on your hearts. Impress them on your children. Talk about them when you sit at home and when you walk along the road, when you lie down and when you get up."*

Women Never Walk without God

It's comforting to know that Jesus also struggled and continues to struggle with rebellious children. After all, our sons and daughters are his sons and daughters, children who disobey and defy even their creator. Furthermore, as mothers we often have that one child who refuses to listen to our words. During those trying moments, all we have to do is pray and ask for the Lord's assistance. *"Lord, I wait for you; you will answer, Lord my God"* Psalm 38:15.

Don't forget, mothers need to be strong because the path is long and often hurdles are many. But, isn't the purpose of mothering the development of a solid, independent adult who truly reflects the image of Christ in thought, word, and deed? I think we all agree that this is the purpose of childbearing and equally, the will of God in fruition. *"That is why a man leaves his father and mother and is united to his wife, and they become one flesh"* Genesis 2:24.

The Purpose: A Mother's Reason to Be

No discipline seems pleasant at the time, but painful. Later on, however, it produces a harvest of righteousness and peace for those who have been trained by it. ~ Hebrews 12:11.

Mothers are not called just to sow seeds, but to fertilize, water, and always pluck out the weeds that obstruct healthy growth. But never forget the value of discipline. Restraint and education must be executed with love and respect. They are vital components in rearing exemplary Christian children. *"Endure hardship as discipline; God is treating you as his children. For what children are not disciplined . . . but God disciplines us for our good, in order that we may share in his holiness . . . No discipline seems pleasant at the time, but painful. Later on, however, it produces a harvest of righteousness and peace for those who have been trained by it"* Hebrews 12:7–11.

Difficult as it may be, I urge all mothers to stop complaining, grumbling, or resorting to name calling when your children disappoint or exasperate you. Instead, turn to God. I handle it by praying. I pause, take a deep breath, and I pray! To fully embrace our maternal purpose and reason to be, we must speak with God, confiding in his infinite goodness. Our children will change and be different if we as mothers follow God and rely on the promises in 2 Peter 1:3: *"His divine power has given us everything we need for a godly life through our knowledge of him who called us by his own glory and goodness."*

Discipline and training are greatly undermined when they are given without respect or affection. Always speak the truth in love when addressing your children, but be firm. *"Whoever spares the rod hates their children, but the one who loves their children is careful to discipline them"* **Proverbs 13:24.**

Mothers, do not fear your tears or your distress. The Lord in his mercy will embrace your unhappiness and frustration; he will understand when you are distraught, and he will accept both your sorrow and restless heart as special prayers for help. Remember, it is in moments of humility and dependence on God that we submit to his will and place our children in his care. Once our sons and daughters are in his hands, he is in charge.

Consequently, with the comfort of divine intercession, we need never fear for the welfare of our children. Never be short on faith. Always be aware that prayer is answered in God's time and in God's way. Nevertheless, it is always answered. *"They all joined together constantly in prayer, along with the women and Mary the mother of Jesus, and with his brothers"* **Acts 1:14.**

CHAPTER SIX

We Pray Because We Are What God Said We Are

God is within her; she will not fall; God will help her at break of day.
~ Psalm 46:5

We Are Partners of the Lord in the Creation of Children
The Lord God said, 'It is not good for the man to be alone. I will make a helper suitable for him.' ~ Genesis 2:18

The question on our lips as women is, are we disappointing the Lord? Are we all that he intended us to be? The following verse in Romans demonstrates that God always loves us, even though we're sinners. *"But God demonstrates his own love for us in this: While we were still sinners, Christ died for us"* Romans 5:8.

In the Old Testament, four centuries before Christ, we read about the reappearance of the Israelites after a seven-decade refuge as expatriates. Upon their return, they reinvented themselves in order to reexperience and discover who they were on a spiritual level, while still battling the generational legacy of God's punishment for sins of the past. But God as divine creator had the upper hand. His plan for us was clear. There was no need for reinvention; the plan of God is unchanging both in time and place.

Did the Lord not make us male and female and in so doing designed gender specific roles? *"The Lord God said, 'It is not good for the man to be alone. I will make a helper suitable for him'"* Genesis 2:18. Thus was defined women's role as wife and mother. *"That is why a man leaves his father and mother and is united to his wife, and they become one flesh"* Genesis 2:24.

In keeping with the divine will, we women are mothers, helpmates, intercessors, nurturers, mediators, referees, fonts of love and compassion, and partners of the Lord in the creation of children. But it doesn't end there. Why? Because we should always be there to rear our offspring, to teach them, to support their endeavors, and above all to pray for them while encouraging them to pray for their own needs and for the strength to grow up to be Christian adults of substance and integrity. Still, our purpose as mothers is forever in evolution.

It is not sufficient to teach, counsel, and guide our children: we must also be a role model, a mission with a wide scope that goes a long way regarding the gains they will reap from our unconditional devotion and loyal commitment.

I have never seen a more richly blessed husband or more abundantly blessed children than those fortunate enough to have a praying wife or mother. King Solomon compares a mother's teaching to a precious piece of jewelry—noticeable and beautiful. But be reminded that once children are grown, they should be able to walk in their own steps, unattended. If not, a mother has failed in her teaching. *"Listen, my son, to your father's instruction and do not forsake your mother's teaching"* Proverbs 1:8. The wise Solomon emphasized the value of a mother's influence in child rearing.

Once children have reached adulthood, a mother has achieved a certain maturity. However, seasoned women have a protocol to follow, not only in maintaining their holiness in God's eyes, but in encouraging younger women to reach their own personal level of godliness. *"Likewise, teach the older women to be reverent in the way they live, not to be slanderers or addicted to much wine, but to teach what is good. Then they can urge the younger women to love their husbands and children to be self-controlled and pure, to be busy at home, to be kind, and to be subject to their husbands, so that no one will malign the word of God"* Titus 2:3–5.

What we teach and how we act should not only impact our children but all with whom we come into contact. This offers special blessings to everyone around us. If as women we practiced this little exercise, just think how many people will be blessed. Furthermore, your strength and your influence will be felt.

Prayer— Love Connection
We love because he first loved us. ~ 1 John 4:19

I wish to return to my original discussion of prayer. We pray because we love, and what we love, we pray for. Never forget, love is born of God and grows on the groundwork of prayer. It is, in a sense, intangible, beyond human control; God alone guides it. Therefore, the love a mother feels for her child surpasses all definitions, is detached from all science of mind and body, is immune to boundary and limit, and fights every foe that tries to interrupt or obstruct its course. *"Can a mother forget her nursing child? Can she feel no love for the child she has born?"* Isaiah 49:15.

The road to love is paved with the same stones as the road to prayer. *"Whoever does not love does not know God, because God is love"* 1 John 4:8. And in Mark 12:30 we are reminded that Jesus himself gave us a commandment: *"Love the Lord your God with all your heart, soul, mind and strength."* How can we as women and mothers love God? We can love him by obeying his commandment and by expressing our love to him, in prayer.

God has given women extra strength: the strength to endure childbirth, the strength to support husbands with compassion and loyalty, and the strength to comfort and nurture children. *"As a mother comforts her child, so will I comfort you"* Isaiah 66:13. A mother's love is so powerful that the Lord uses it as a metaphor in his messages.

We are very strong. This is how God has made us, so please let's not give up on our husbands, our children, and even our loved ones. Prayer changes everything, so let's just be patient and keep trusting the Lord.

As most of you know, this special divine strength is our lifesaver. To love is not as easy as it may seem. *"Love is patient, love is kind. It does not envy, it does not boast, it is not proud. It does not dishonor others, it is not self-seeking, it is not easily angered, it keeps no record of wrongs. Love does not delight in evil but rejoices with the truth. It always protects, always trusts, always hopes, always perseveres"* 1 Corinthians 13:4–7. These beautiful words and equally beautifully expressions of a sentiment are given in instruction, though at times are not an easy teaching. Here is where prayer enters!

But let us never forget: *"From everyone who has been given much, much will be demanded; and from the one who has been entrusted with much, much more will be asked"* Luke 12:48.

I will conclude this chapter with the words of 1 Peter 3:1–6, which clearly convey the Lord's intentions for women. *"Wives, in the same way submit yourselves to your own husbands so that, if any of them do not believe the word, they may be won over without words by the behavior of their wives, when they see the purity and reverence of your lives. Your beauty should not come from outward adornment, such as elaborate hairstyles and the wearing of gold jewelry or fine clothes. Rather, it should be that of your inner self, the unfading beauty of a gentle and quiet spirit, which is of great worth in God's sight. For this is the way the holy women of the past who put their hope in God used to adorn themselves. They submitted themselves to their own husbands, like Sarah, who obeyed Abraham and called him her lord."*

Such is the will of God for us!

CHAPTER SEVEN

We Pray Because We Have Challenges

And I have promised to bring you up out of your misery in Egypt into the land of the Canaanites, Hittites, Amorites, Perizzites, Hivites and Jebusites—a land flowing with milk and honey.
~ *Exodus 3:17*

What If, as Women, We Hold the Hand of God While Crossing the Battlefield?
You intended to harm me, but God intended it for good to accomplish what is now being done, the saving of many lives.
~ Genesis 50:20

The way to reach the Lord is to walk along the path of the mind. This may sound complicated, but in reality, it is simple. Just a thought about God taking your hand during a challenging moment is a declaration of faith—a prayer. And the divine promise is to answer our prayers. *"Now to him who is able to do immeasurably more than all we ask or imagine, according to his power that is at work within us"* Ephesians 3:20. Therefore, I urge all women and mothers to go forward in the direction of the Lord, feeling assured he will undoubtedly take you by the hand, assuming you move onward in faith, and with trust in your heart.

In the Old Testament we meet a woman, Jochebed, the birth mother of Moses, who sacrificed for the safety of her child. She devised a plan that would entail giving up her son to keep him alive. In the end the Lord blessed her for her deed, as she was chosen to nurse the same baby, the infant she placed in a papyrus-layered basket after she slathered him in pitch. The basket was put adrift along the banks of the Nile and his salvation left to God. *"So, the girl went and got the baby's mother. Pharaoh's daughter said to her, 'Take this baby and nurse him for me, and I will pay you.' So, the woman took the baby and nursed him. When the child grew older, she took him to Pharaoh's daughter and he became her son. She named him Moses, saying, 'I drew him out of the water.'"* Exodus 2:9–10.

Life presents challenges for all. Obstacles and recurrent oppositions are part of the earthly journey, as are sacrifices, agony, and feelings of despair. Did not Hannah pray? We all recognize how compelling her situation was: *"There was a certain man from Ramathaim, a Zuphite from the hill country of Ephraim, whose name was Elkanah son of Jeroham, the son of Elihu, the son of Tohu, the son of Zuph, an Ephraimite. He had two wives; one was called Hannah and the other Peninnah. Peninnah had children, but Hannah had none.*

*Year after year this man went up from his town to worship and sacrifice to the L*ORD *Almighty at Shiloh, where Hophni and Phinehas, the two sons of Eli, were priests of the L*ORD*. Whenever the day came for Elkanah to sacrifice, he would give portions of the meat to his wife Peninnah and to all her sons and daughters. But to Hannah he gave a double portion because he loved her"* 1 Samuel 1:1–5.

But Hannah's story does not end there. *"The Lord had closed her womb!"* 1 Samuel 1:6. Therein was the woman's devastation. However, distraught and filled with sorrow, Hannah neither lost faith nor surrendered to defeat. Instead, if we continue to read 1 Samuel 1, we learn that *"In her deep anguish Hannah prayed to the Lord, weeping bitterly. And she made a vow, saying, 'Lord Almighty, if you will only look on your servant's misery and remember me, and not forget your servant but give her a son, then I will give him to the Lord for all the days of his life, and no razor will ever be used on his head.'"* 1 Samuel 1:10–11.

Hannah's persistence continued. She prayed herself out using every bit of strength in her. *"I am a woman who is deeply troubled. I have not been drinking wine or beer; I was pouring out my soul to the Lord. Do not take your servant for a wicked woman; I have been praying here out of my great anguish and grief"* 1 Samuel 1:15–16. As always, the Lord heard the prayers of a woman in pain and anguish. *"So, in the course of time Hannah became pregnant and gave birth to a son. She named him Samuel, saying, 'Because I asked the Lord for him'"* 1 Samuel 1:20. Such is the power of prayer either spoken or in silence, but in blind faith.

Prayer Is the Answer

But when you pray, go into your room, close the door and pray to your Father, who is unseen. Then your Father, who sees what is done in secret, will reward you. ~ Matthew 6:6–7

Juggling families and careers, we will always have challenges throughout our earthly existence. Who among us enjoys sunny skies, calm seas, and smooth sailing 365 days of the year? If there is someone, I would certainly like to meet her! As we all know from experience, life itself is a challenge. Nevertheless, as Christian women and mothers, we should always be ready to pray with every breath we breathe, because the truth is, we will always run into conflicts and situational disagreements with our husbands and children. These clashes, if permitted, will impede us from living happy, successful, and fulfilled lives.

Once again, I can never sufficiently emphasize that in times of distress, in times of frustration and confusion, the best solution for overcoming obstacles that block serenity is prayer. You just have to keep praying until all your energy seeps out: Run to the throne, not to the phone. Take your troubles to the Lord, not to your friends. There is only one trusted confidante—Jesus Christ. *"But he said to me, 'My grace is sufficient for you, for my power is made perfect in weakness.' Therefore, I will boast all the more gladly about my weaknesses, so that Christ's power may rest on me"* 2 Corinthians 12:9.

His understanding, his compassion, and his empathy are incomparable, and his promise to listen never wavers. I cite this passage quite frequently because it carries a reassuring promise. *"As a mother comforts her child, so will I comfort you; and you will be comforted over Jerusalem"* Isaiah 66:13.

CHAPTER EIGHT

We Pray Because We Love

Prayer can be a seed sown in the lives of our children, which manifests in them as they grow in the way of the Lord.
~ *Salome Ikem*

Love and Faith Dismiss Doubts

I command you: be strong and steadfast! Do not fear nor be dismayed, for the Lord, your God, is with you wherever you go.
~ Joshua 1:9

The passage from 1 Corinthians 13:4–5, cited in chapter six, says it all. We as women and mothers must be patient when asking God for favors. We must place full trust in his promise to hear our prayers while believing our past requests will be heard. Love is what helps us to be patient. Love is healing, inspiring, and comforting. Love is encouraging and inspirational, redemptive and pardoning, a necessity of life. *"Dear friends, let us love one another, for love comes from God. Everyone who loves has been born of God and knows God"* 1 John 4:7. Therefore I tell you—never give up on love.

If you recall, in chapter seven I discussed Hannah's insistent prayers for a child, recorded in 1 Samuel 1. Tenacious and determined, she never ceased addressing the Lord. Instead, she went up to the temple and prayed in tears, promising to give her son to the service of the Lord if her request would be granted. *"As she kept on praying to the Lord, Eli observed her mouth. Hannah was praying in her heart, and her lips were moving but her voice was not heard. Eli thought she was drunk and said to her, 'How long are you going to stay drunk? Put away your wine'"* 1 Samuel 1:12–14. Hannah continued to pray because she desired to give birth to a son. When a woman has faith, her love gives her grace to pray, and the strength and trust to await God's will.

Women Are Love
The Lord expects us to love everyone, even those with whom we may be at variance, cross, in disagreement, or disappointed with for whatever motive. *"Love is patient, love is kind, it does not envy, it does not boast, it is not proud, it does not dishonor others, it is not self-seeking, it is not easily angered, it keeps no record of wrongs"* 1 Corinthians 13:4–5.

Isn't it true that sometimes it is more agreeable and easier to fire anger at another, instead of kindling them with the fire of our love? The more difficult the relationship, the more challenging is the willingness to love, and consequently the more worthy the love. *"Do everything in love"* 1 Corinthians 16:14.

The Lord expects us to be meek and mild in demeanor, unassuming and completely humble and kind, as well as tolerant and enduring, with all who cross our paths.

Be aware that there is no fear in love. Above all, love each other deeply, because love covers over a multitude of sins, and no man or woman walking the earth is free of sin. Therefore, never ridicule a woman praying for what she loves because she is both focused on the Lord and determined to have her favor granted. Fully realizing that doubts are gone when in humble prayer, she pauses often during her busy day to have a word with the Lord.

Women are wise. Scientists have proven that women can think faster than men, therefore we are not afraid to pray for what we love, knowing that we have thought about it before praying.

This gift of wisdom gives us the insights and the willingness to bow our heads. Why? Because we have dedicated much thought to our intentions before offering prayers.

One Woman's Prayer Saved a Nation

Do not be anxious about anything, but in every situation, by prayer and petition, with thanksgiving, present your requests to God. And the peace of God, which transcends all understanding, will guard your hearts and your minds in Christ Jesus. ~ Philippians 4:6–7

There is no defeat in prayer. Esther put all her trust in God and prayed to become a queen. Through prayer and fasting for three days, she begged God to set her nation free. Aware that going uninvited before the king could cost her life, she waited patiently for the right moment to plead for the life of her people. "*'If it pleases the king,' she said, 'and if he regards me with favor and thinks it the right thing to do, and if he is pleased with me, let an order be written overruling the dispatches that Haman son of Hammedatha, the Agagite, devised and wrote to destroy the Jews in all the king's provinces'*" Esther 8:5. Esther was a woman of great faith with the courage to fully live it. Don't just read about Esther—be Esther. There is no reason why you cannot be an Esther in today's world!

A woman of faith holds power with the Lord. Never forget these words, but repeat them during the day, especially during trying moments when the easiest option seems to be quitting. Think of the passage in Matthew 9:20–23 that speaks of a woman with a severe bleeding problem who, thanks to her faith and courage in approaching the Lord, was relieved of her debilitating malady.

Tenacious and obstinate, she braced herself to cut through the crowd that tried to stop her, to get to Jesus, praying in good faith for the miracles she wanted. Her goal was to touch the cloak of Jesus. *"Just then a woman who had been subject to bleeding for twelve years came up behind him and touched the edge of his cloak. She said to herself, 'If I only touch his cloak, I will be healed.' Jesus turned and saw her. 'Take heart, daughter,' he said, 'your faith has healed you.' And the woman was healed at that moment"* Matthew 9:20–22.

We should never be too tired or too hungry, neither should we be too stressed to address the Lord in good conscience. However, much as prayer is our greatest ally as women and mothers, and much as the Lord has compassion and mercy for a woman kneeling in prayer, reading the creator's messages and teaching in the Bible, we learn that prayer that is not followed by a good faith deed or action can evaporate into thin air. In other words, we must do our part to attain our goals, and the Lord will assist through all the challenging hurdles.

In the sacred Scripture, there is certainly no deficit of courageous women to hold in high regard. Take for instance Abigail, a perfect example of beauty and brains. We read in 1 Samuel 25 how she used her wisdom along with her wealth to plead for the safety of her husband's household. Meanwhile, David, the future king of Israel, swore to seek vengeance after being insulted by Nabal, but was so moved by Abigail's humble plea that his heart turned. David said to Abigail, *"Praise be to the Lord, the God of Israel, who has sent you today to meet me. May you be blessed for your good judgment and for keeping me from bloodshed this day and from avenging myself with my own hands"* 1 Samuel 25:32–33.

Show me a successful man, and I will show you a praying wife; show me children of excellence, and I will also show you a praying mother. *"She is clothed with strength and dignity; she can laugh at the days to come. She speaks with wisdom, and faithful instruction is on her tongue"* Proverbs 31:25–26.

CHAPTER NINE

We Pray Because We Need God

We have to realize that by ourself we are weak, it is only Christ that strengthens us: He is our refuge and our fortress. With God, we always have security.
~ *Salome Ikem*

Prayer Is a Conversation with God
The Lord is near to all who call on Him, to all who call on Him in truth. ~ Psalm 145:18

God is near to those who call out to him, those who call him with sincerity and love in their hearts. During these unsettled, turbulent times, we need God more than ever. No one has the love for us that the Lord demonstrates. No one possesses either compassion or the willingness to forgive as he does. He is truly our refuge and our fortress. In him there is always the promise of security and safety.

As in every meaningful relationship, communication is in a sense the life force. Without dialogue, even the apparently strongest liaison will crumble. Consequently, if women wish to grow in their union with the Lord, they must speak to him openly, trustingly, and in good faith. Regardless of how successful women are, they absolutely cannot cross the threshold and overcome the obstacles of life alone, without divine assistance. *"God is our refuge and strength, an ever-present help in trouble. Therefore, we will not fear, though the earth gives way and the mountains fall into the heart of the sea"* Psalm 46:1–2.

Prayer assures us that the line of communication remains open with God. In essence, our dialogue is a discussion with him regarding our needs and wants. Perhaps even more importantly, it is a moment to just acknowledge our relationship with the Lord, and to express our thanks for blessings received. In other words, prayer is simply an exchange of words with God.

We must speak to our Father at all times. Why? Because it is impossible to serenely continue along the paths of our life journey unaccompanied by our Savior. *"He is our very heartbeat. The Lord is near to all who call on him, to all who call on him in truth. He fulfills the desires of those who fear him; he hears their cry and saves them"* Psalm 145:18–19

God listens to all who call him. Who among us has not felt alone, misunderstood, and perhaps powerless in trying to overcome our daily life challenges? And who has not felt the refuge of the Lord after crying out to him possibly even in desperation? *"The name of the Lord is a strong tower; the righteous run into it and are safe"* Proverbs 18:10.

In today's troubled times, with the COVID-19 pandemic and the devastating racial conflicts that are tearing us further from the Lord's teaching, we must go to him humbly, asking for mercy and for the willingness to humbly comply with his wishes for us. Who, after all, knows the desires of our hearts, the thoughts in our minds, and the needs of our bodies and souls better than he who created us?

And who in return asks us to imitate his love and respect for our universal brothers and sisters? *"A new command I give you: Love one another. As I have loved you, so you must love one another. By this everyone will know that you are my disciples, if you love one another"* John 13:34–35.

Let us look to Esther's courage in stepping up to a challenge, Judith's bold belief-based convictions and unrelenting determination, and Deborah's power in a judicial seat. How successful, how influential were these women, and how faithfully they all prayed to their Lord for assistance and solidarity. And what of Mary, the mother of Jesus? How strong was her faith in God to accept such a special mission at so vulnerable an age?

Just imagine for a moment how powerful her words were in conversing with her creator. Mary needed God. She could not walk that special journey alone. Yet she had the courage to trust, an act of faith that altered the course of humanity. We also must dialogue with the Lord, open our hearts to him, discuss our problems, our sadness, our heartaches and disappointments, our needs. Likewise, we must never forget to mention to him gratitude for our joy and blessings, our husbands and children, and all the abundance we enjoy within our hearts.

The Lord is our only salvation! If humanity is not willing or does not otherwise understand, they will face the consequences. In the Lord there is not only redemption and salvation, but security and serenity. Alone we can do nothing. The Lord is our mind and our heart. He is every word we say, every step we take, every smile we smile, and every tear we shed. Without him our hearts cease to beat and our minds to think. He is our life force. *"I can do all things through Christ who strengthens me"* Philippians 4:13.

Do not be anxious about anything, but in everything, by prayer and petition, with thanksgiving, present your requests to God.
~ Philippians 4:6

AFTERWORD

We are in a very difficult moment at present with unrest in the world, a seemingly unconstrained COVID pandemic, and fearful inklings of an unsettling future as a possible legacy for our children, should God continue to be censored. However, challenges and adversity are not new to the world. The Bible narrates of previous disconcerting times where all seemed hopeless and desperate. God, however, promised hope to the believer regardless of his plight. *"For in this hope we were saved. But hope that is seen is no hope at all. Who hopes for what they already have?"* Romans 8:24. Nevertheless, in response to prayer, mankind has survived, fueled by the grace of God.

To know someone, it is essential to spend time conversing with them, exchanging ideas and sharing feelings. Knowledge of the Lord is the seed of love. *"I no longer call you servants, because a servant does not know his master's business. Instead, I have called you friends, for everything that I learned from my Father I have made known to you"* John 15:15. So it is with God.

May every woman who prays discover the glory, intercession, and assistance of blessings received as I have and continue to be granted. Have faith, love instead of chastising others, and PRAY: All prayers are answered in the Lord's timing. Be not timid, be not fearful—he awaits.

I asked, and I was given my husband and my children; I pursued and I discovered; I knocked and we were welcomed; I PRAYED and Jesus stepped into my home and my life!

Whoever does not love does not know God, because God is love.
~ 1 John 4:8.

www.ingramcontent.com/pod-product-compliance
Lightning Source LLC
Chambersburg PA
CBHW071751040426
42446CB00012B/2520